MOM, I made you a BOOK

DEAR **MOM**,

I made this book for you because you're a great mom. Thank you for ALL that you do and ALL the ways you help me grow. I've included some of them here in these pages, but there are just TOO MANY to fit into one book. I made this ESPECIALLY for you because you really are ONE OF A KIND.

Love, ____________

HERE'S ME!

MOM, YOU MAKE OUR FAMILY A

family.

WE LOVE EACH OTHER A LOT!

HERE, I DREW A PICTURE OF

us together.

You're great at making our days together SPECIAL, right from the start.

You help me get ready for my day by:

I see how much you provide for me. From the clothes that I wear to the food that I eat, you make sure I have just what I need.

HERE'S A LIST OF THINGS YOU'VE GIVEN ME, JUST TO NAME A FEW:

Thanks to you,
I'm very SMART.

If you asked me,
I could count
as high as
this number:

That's how many

I'd like to give you.

I'm SO proud that you're my mom. I'd show you off to anyone!

I'll even introduce you to THIS CAT:

Excuse me, cat. Let me tell you about my mom.
She loves _____.
She's AMAZING at _____.
And she makes me feel IMPORTANT by _____.
Bye!

YOU'RE EXACTLY
THE PERFECT
MOM FOR ME
BECAUSE...

You believe in me no matter what, even when I'm:

(check the boxes)

You help me be my BEST by

____.

So, here's a

BIG THANK-YOU HIGH FIVE

for being so awesome.

(TRACE HAND)

You deserve a gazillion MORE!

We really do know each other well.

I like that you know my favorite food is:

And I know that you really like:

Together we do
SO MANY FUN things!

Here's my favorite thing we do INSIDE

and my favorite thing we do OUTSIDE!

I have lots of happy memories with you!

Here's a picture of us when we

____

____

so we can always remember.

I just Love you..
(check the boxes)
□ Kisses
□ Snuggles
□ READING TOGETHER

..Here are a few ways I like to show you that:

☐ MAKING ART for you

☐ Hugs

☐

(WRITE YOUR OWN!)

HERE, LET ME GIVE YOU THIS AWARD.

WORLD'S
MOM

Thank you, Mom.
Because of you, I know that:

(check the boxes)

- ☐ You are always there for me
- ☐ We'll have lots more ADVENTURES
- ☐ I AM LOVED
- ☐ You help me be ME
- ☐ (WRITE YOUR OWN!)

BECAUSE OF YOU, WE ARE A FAMILY.

Compendium
live inspired

Actually written by:

- - - - - - - - - -

Write your name!

Written by: Miriam Hathaway
Illustrated by: Asahi Nagata
Edited by: Bailey Vega
Art Directed by: Justine Edge

ISBN: 978-1-957891-46-0

1st printing. Printed in China with soy inks on FSC®-Mix certified paper. A012409001

Create meaningful moments with gifts that inspire.

CONNECT WITH US
live-inspired.com | sayhello@compendiuminc.com

@compendiumliveinspired
#compendiumliveinspired